CW00525735

poems for

Wonderland

First published 2024 by The Hedgehog Poetry Press

Published in the UK by
The Hedgehog Poetry Press
5, Coppack House
Churchill Avenue
Clevedon
BS21 6QW

www.hedgehogpress.co.uk

ISBN: 978-1-916830-10-3

9 8 7 6 5 4 3 2 1

A CIP Catalogue record for this book is available from the British
Library.

Original illustrations by John Tenniel, Public Domain with thanks to
RawPixel

poems for

Wonderland

Contents:

PHILIPPA HATTON-LEPINE

how doth the little white rabbit

how doth the little white rabbit
work with hardly a break
although he often delegates
and dare not make mistakes

who is the little white rabbit
no-one knows his real name
the person he was this morning
will always be the same

he's never tried to talk to time
one day it will run out
he will forever be late then
of that there is no doubt

buried with his beloved watch
to mock him night and day
he'll rest just like a child's soft toy
discarded after play

perhaps we are flames on candles
burning bright for a spell
where do we go when we're blown out
this only time will tell

(based on How Doth the Little Busy Bee by Isaac Watts and How Doth the Little Crocodile by Lewis Carroll)

RHIANNON LEWIS

Time for Tea

Time ticking by,
I am a slave to it,
To the habitual ritual of it,
The cups and saucers,
The seating and place settings,
The water and morsels to eat.

Time is ticking by,
And whatever time it is,
It's always time for a tea party,
And I've grown to really dislike teatime.

I'm standing around,
I'm picked up and put down,
I'm hot, I'm cold,
I need topping up.

And all that chatter from the Mad Hatter,
He can talk and talk and talk and talk...
Making unending cups of tea,
Is difficult with a dormouse living inside me.

It's teatime all the time,
And I've grown to really dislike teatime.

MARGARET ROYALL

In which Alice and the Cheshire Cat meet the Three-tailed squirrel

Alice:
You really shouldn't hang about in trees, you know,
it's rude to scare folk as they wander past.
No doubt you think you're a very clever cat,
doling out your pearls of wisdom..... well, Mr High and-Mighty,

let me put you right about that;
it's downright patronising, arrogant in fact.
I asked a simple question. You answered me with riddles...
now what's the point of that?

Don't just sit there grinning at me.... and
don't start hissing, showing me your teeth.
You 're just a fat marmalade sandwich, a sloth.
Whoever heard of Cheshire anyway?

Three-tailed squirrel:
Excuse me, Miss, I overheard your argument
Can I assist in settling this dispute?

Alice:
And tell me, pray who are you?
You've got three tails, a little strange,
but maybe three brains in your head too?

Three-tailed squirrel:
I'm Percy, the wise, the bold, the scary,
best judge in all of Wonderland.
You'd better pay me well though, for I can bite!

Alice:
Be off with you, or I'll show you what for!
I'll call the Queen and she'll shout *off with his head!*
You're both of you too boastful and make no sense at all.

Cheshire Cat:
Oh please stop all this shouting!
It's time for my nap and you're keeping me awake.
Go where you please, do what you want,
I really couldn't care less.

Three-tailed squirrel:
He's just a marmalade sandwich, a sloth!
Come on, let's go and join the fun.
I hear the Mad Hatter's bash is quite the thing!

PHIL SANTUS

What Alice learned

As Alice says: some things come easily:
the light suffused across the world,
the green shoots rising up in springtime.

As Alice says: the world is a curious place,
no need for rabbit holes to enter wonderlands,
wonder is everywhere, you only need to interact.

As Alice says: there is a child within us all,
who needs to seek and needs to find,
and who needs to have their adventures.

As Alice knows: we were always meant to be,
existence makes it so, but still we must discover
who we are and what we want to be.

JENNIFER SCHNEIDER

Wonder Meter

2. Lie is 1° removed from life. True or False.
3. Life is more angular than circular. True or False.
5. What word is missing from the following list?
    Maze. Amaze. Wonder. Wander.
6. One more day or one more love. Choose one.
7. Shooting stars have memory. True or False.
8. Wander precedes Wonder. True or False.
9. Wonder follows Thunder. True or False.
10. Define climax.
11. Spades precede Hearts. True or False.
12. All plots have points. True or False.
14. All points have plots. True or False.
15. Does memory hold meaning?
16. Beyond coffee what brews daily?
17. Numbered days are arbitrary. True or False.
28. Calendars are created, not curated. True or False.
29. S _ UD. What letter is missing?
30. At what age did you stop believing in the tooth fairy?
32. At what age did you begin to question destiny?
34. How many days remain in the bank?
35. Mirrors reveal truths. True or False.
36. Clubs are more valuable than diamonds. True or False.
38. Is truth telling?
40. Wonder is quantifiable. True or False.

Wonder Meter Calculation:

- For all True responses, add one point.
- For all False responses, deduct one point.
- For all questions answered instinctively, add the question value to the running total.
- If you've come this far and wonder about the point of this plot, return to Question 1.

KATE YOUNG

Nothing but a Pack of Cards

'Twas puddlesome that dreichan day
So Alice, feeling doldigloom
Decided to skittle off and play,
A new adventure to consume.

It wasn't long before she tumbled
Down yet another scrumpled hole,
Emerged conflabbled, somewhat crumpled
And met a miser-whiskered mole.

"You're early" wheezed an oily voice
While pouring tea onto the table
"I'd show you round myself, but sadly,
With my poor sight I am not able."

"I'm waiting for the deck of spades
To shuffle in and dig me out.
You're a jack-of-all-trades, Alice
Help me!" But Alice began to shout

And stomp, a proper old paddyscreechum
That made the Ace come nimblequick
And drag the girl, so wearisome
Into a pool of mudderslick.

When she emerged her hair all squiggled
In grizzled strands of mud and oil,
The spades began to clank and giggle
But Alice was feeling furyboil.

She scraped and clawed along the dirt
Past the Clubs and all their guards,
She surfaced, dungy, but quite unhurt,
"You're nothing but a pack of cards!"

GRETA ROSS

Those Pesky Oranges

(inspired by Prokofiev's opera libretto 'The Love for Three Oranges' and Lewis Carroll's 'Alice in Wonderland')

The populace is lamenting the sickness of the Prime Minister brought on by an indulgence in tragic poetry. There lies the wan PM, immersed in the verbal swamps and heaves of T.S. Eliot's The Wasteland. Oh the misery, oh the heartache of the wanderer in that land of Waste, the great man weeps. He cries out *Shanti Shanti Shanti* in a shimmer of spiritualism before realising the prayer is Hindu and he is in the wrong continent. *Damn that Eliot* he shouts and throws his tome of worthy poetry into the fireplace warming his stately bedroom. As if by magic the beautiful goddess Pomona, clad in fiery robes, springs out of the flames. In her hand are three perfect oranges, which she proceeds to juggle faultlessly. The PM, awestruck not by her beauty but by her circus skills, grabs the oranges. What a woman can do he, the pinnacle of the nation, can doubtlessly do far better. As if by a miracle all thoughts of poetry flee his brain and he feels revived, but somehow troublingly cosmopolitan, and – God forbid – European. His mind traipses through the EU, confused to hear Pomona shout out different names for mere oranges.

> Sanskrit *naranga*
> mutates in Italy
> to *arancia*
>
> Lisbon's *laranja*
> is reborn Spain's *naranja*
> but all taste the same

No wonder border checks take so long, the great leader thinks. Dropping an orange for the nth time, he develops a crippling migraine and has to lie down again. His faithful fool, Pantaloon, in bow tie and striped waistcoat, thrusts a new book of poetry at him, this time by wild-eyed Blake with tales of Hell and its demons. Unnoticed, the fallen orange slowly splits open. A not-so-young damsel rises, her hair a blazing crimson. It is the Red Queen. She reads her lines from a parchment scroll in her hands: *oh ye foolish lump, behold before thee a princess, nay Queen, all super-pure and proclaimed wonderful by me!* His mind still buzzing from the migraine, the PM raises an eyebrow. He is deep in communion with Blake's spectral angels and devils and suspects this apparition is one of that vile cohort. He tosses the ravaged orange peel at her: *Away! In what furnace was thy brain? Do you not see I am on my Couch of Death? Away!*

The Red Queen spits out a pip and approaches the PM and his fool. The endgame approaches.

> Her saffron robe slips
> fruity abundance dazzles
> both men fall struck dumb

GWEN SAYERS

How to Catch a March Hare

Lounge on a sage green couch,
garbed in puffed sleeves and pinny.
Forget the skulk of foxes, knot
of toads. Line a nest with fluff
shed from the hare's scut.

Offer him chamomile tea,
thistle tart and marsh mallow
sprinkled with sorrel. Stroke
his donkey-ears. Kiss his muzzle.
Garland his wrists

with bands woven from ivy.
If he leaps towards grease wood
tether him to a lime tree, hum
siren melodies until he forgets
who he used to be.

When his wide, glassy eyes glaze,
loosen his waistcoat and bow tie,
slip a straw wreath around his head.
If he still snuffles for freedom
present him with a cradle of bunnies.

BEVERLY FRYDMAN

Call Me Mrs White Rabbit

Falling towards London on a 747   the plane drops then settles my
unzipped handbag spills   tampons a hairbrush   just in case panties
onto size ten loafers belonging to my beloved   busy jiggling his legs and
checking his watch   mini g&t bottles tumble into my lap   they plead
with me   *drink us now*   I stuff them in my pocket for later   we land
with a thud   some people applaud and thank the lord   then mass
unbuckling   everyone's standing   my husband's scampering down the
aisle   my purse on his shoulder   iPhone glued to his ear   he's
unaware I'm nowhere near   still in my seat I gather up   lipstick on
deep breath in   my husband first to the exit door   I hear him rabbiting
on and on   imploring the stewardess or heavens above   to open the
doors   let him out of the gate   *for god's sake please   I'm late   I'm late*

DAVID PUNTER

An Ecological Fantasy

I met an aged, aged man
a-sitting on a gate
he said I must go catch my bus
or else I shall be late

I said there are no buses here
for this is Wonderland
he said if you could pay my fare
why, that would be well grand

And then a bus did come along
a strange sight to my eyes
with curious creatures all a-glint
and all of different size

Is that a turtle I behold
beside a lonesome griffin
mice are sitting next to cats
getting along just spiffing

Maybe (I thought) this is just like
the world beyond the stream
that separates our life from death
(but this is just a dream

Of how the animals and us
might share the world alike -
the rich man in his royce of rolls
the poor man on his bike)

We all could get along somehow -
that's how so many taught us
before that dreadful accident
when surplus profit bought us.

DAWN GORMAN

And later /Alice / you will fall again /

lean your woman's body into a new slow-motion plunge through space /
reach out not for jars on passing shelves / but for a person / online /
and be amazed once more how far / and how deep / you will go /
and the doors to the garden will have simply become screens
where you'll type things that matter / swap stories / drink him in /
then you'll Zoom / see a smile / not in the sky / but in the intimate glow
of your laptop / and although living so far apart will be frustrating /
you'll remember how one thing can always become another /
so when he shares a video of himself playing croquet / you'll just
close your eyes / imagine you're there / and slip into the scene /
feel the sun / sweet as desire on your skin / and know that the crowd
standing between you are fiction / cards from a deck / so you'll tap one /
they'll all tumble / and you'll laugh as you realise you were right
all along / *very few things indeed were really impossible* / and you'll
walk through the scent of white roses to meet the touch of his fingers /
then Alice / oh Alice / you'll be falling / together / in wonder

RUSSELL E. WILLIS

Painting the Roses Red

I've always loved red roses.
So, when told to paint the white ones red,
I didn't even wonder if this
Was something I should do.

But, once the paint was dripping
And all I smelled was paint,
It dawned on me that not to wonder, in this land,
Might be a weakness and not a strength.

Realizing that I like white roses, too,
Simply did not help. For not only
Wonder had been banished, but memory as well,
Not to mention reason.

So, when told to paint the white ones red,
I didn't even wonder.

TINA MACNAUGHTON

Mirror, mirror

mirror, mirror make me tall   how much farther if I fall?
eat me, drink me, take my hand   running, catch me if you can

dream or madness, end's the start   how long 'til she breaks my heart?
double trouble, mind the cat   grinning sideways, where's he at?
pouring, snoring, tea is served   welcome to un-birthday world

topsy-turvy or absurd   is this madness?

      shhh...
              ...seen not heard.

KERRY DARBISHIRE

What would you give

to never leave a land of creatures
    who charm us through our sleep? The ones
who won't, the ones who will, the ones
    with claws and teeth,

the curious, ridiculous, and the ones who know it all?

To follow the upways the downways the sideways
    and new ways to the cat grinning wider than sky,
tell me what would you say to the owl and a panther
    quietly sharing a pie?

What would you give to talk with poor souls

with a habit of making us small, or the tall and clumsy,
    the card-thin judgementals or Queens who instead
yell *off with her head!* And what would you give to share
    with a Hare, Hatter, and Dormouse drowning in tea,

and the sometimes creatures squandering stars who live

at the edge of the sea? To dream forever to the lull
    of rock pools, a Mock Turtle sobbing away
and dance with a Gryphon the Lobster Quadrille,
    what would you give to stay?

PATRICIA M OSBORNE

Seahorse Brigade

The Grandfather clock strikes three,
my shoes squeak on the gleaming tiles,
sounds echo in the empty museum.

Drawn to a giant's throne hulking
in the corner of the room, I climb
up on the divan-sized seat,
finger armrest engravings,
press a clip underneath –

The floor rises to a new level. I'm in a doorless lift,
gaze down to the ground at a floor length Ludo board.

Stomps echo in the high-rise chamber.
Heels clap together. A thumping pain springs
to my chest as an overgrown red seahorse soldier
wearing jackboots marches in my direction.

The soldier moves closer, his black eyes swing
like a clock pendulum. He steps on red circles
towards *Home*, and *Home* just happens to be me.

He blows a whistle. Twenty or more of the platoon
parade out. Reds, blues, greens and yellows stand
to attention on their rightful squares. My hand shaking,
I press the lever on the chair. I must return home.

No, it whisks me with the whole squad down to a beach.
More soldiers wade from the sea and surround me.

The regiment splits in two to form an aisle. A green t*rumpeteer*
plays the Royal Entrance Fanfare while the rest fold into a bow.

I glance upwards as the seahorse queen struts down the path
singing *Off with his head,* and the drums join in. My heart bangs
in time to the drummers' beat. *I wish I had a cup of tea.*

CHRIS HEMINGWAY

Visit Cheshire Tribunal

The man who was sacked from the Tourist Board
could see nothing wrong.
'Come to Cheshire' he said
'the land of cheese that crumbles,
and cats who disappear,
leaving only their smiles behind.'

The man who was sacked from the Tourist Board
waved Jodrell Bank tea towels
at the stoney-faced panel.
'Emphasising the impermanent you say?
These telescopes track sound
from cat-smile constellations.
Mews and murmurs, across the millennia.'

Then sensing it was time,
he broke into a rhyme;
'You knew when you employed me
my only gift is nonsense verse,
Given as a blessing.
Taken as a curse.
If I was a walrus
and you all worked with wood.
I'm sure my explanations
would be clearly understood',

'Sorry' said the panel chair
'it's good but way off brand.
This is Alan Garner Country.
A different Wonderland.

ISABEL MILES

Sympathy for the Jabberwock

I get so tired of endless knights:
their antics fail to thrill me.
I'd rather read a book than fight
dimwits who try to kill me.

Each morning, when I take my walk,
the noise I make attracts them.
They hide in bushes, jeer and gawk,
though I do not attack them.

They whack me, but I pay no mind,
and disregard their lances.
For my scales are the hard, tough kind,
off which sharp steel just glances.

I'm vegan, and I eat each day,
enormous mounds of carrots,
mostly washed down with Beaujolais,
sometimes with fine old claret,

which sets my tummy burbling.
It pains me much to mention
the sound folk find so threatening
is chronic indigestion.

It's nice and quiet this afternoon.
The knights must all be resting.
They always come back far too soon⁻
it's really rather testing.

Just as I'm thinking, 'Peace at last',
along comes yet another,
a small one, and not very fast.
I wonder why they bother.

He's just a lad. I'm not afraid
since I'm a near-immortal
who can't be harmed by common blade.
Oh dear! That sword looks vorpal.

CASSIA STEVENS

Not Strictly Dancing

I get such a thrill from a lobster quadrille
But I feel I want to branch out,
Dancing is freedom, no strictures, no limits,
Let's dive down to the seabed and scout.

A quick look about, 'twixt coral and sea grass,
The crustaceans are ready and waiting,
Lycra and spray tans, sequins and can cans
It's the show we've all been anticipating

Come dancing my lovelies, don't be afraid
The judges will mostly be kind,
Craig will be sour, he will pout and he will glower
He's the panto baddie defined.

Here come the scallops gyrating in samba
The langoustines do the lambada
Not far behind them a squid does a rumba
And the shrimp perform a cha cha cha!

Oysters are waltzing, their footwork fantastic
And in the sea kelp the clams do a tango
Mussels can quickstep and cockles can foxtrot
And a cuttlefish does the fandango

Abalones & sea urchins, winkles and whelks
In wonderful, perfect formation
They writhe and they jive, their footwork sublime,
It's a perfect 10 from the whole of the nation.

SHARRON GREEN

Down the Rabbit Hole

The loss of childhood innocence
is such a tragedy.
Life's challenges become immense
when you hit puberty.

Your body changes, and your mood,
there is no solid ground.
You get upset, are often rude,
and baffle those around.

The world you enter makes no sense,
so filled with silly riddles,
and adult logic is so dense,
corrupted by their fiddles.

Danger and risk lurk everywhere,
they plague the path you tread,
for even if you do take care,
you could still end up dead.

Alice in Wonderland explains
the agony of growing pains.

CEINWEN E CARIAD HAYDON

Incongruities (after How doth the little crocodile)

How does my swishy lover-boy
Lend sunshine to my days?
His kisses give me sparkly joy,
He's sure I'll sing his praise.
In spite of all this zingy sex,
I feel quite uneasy.
Freaked out, I read his private texts,
then grasp he's using me.

STEPHEN BONE

The Mad Hatter's Nightmare

How it happened is beyond me.
One minute I'm sipping a fine Indian blend
with the Dormouse and March Hare and the next,
I'm in this nonsensical world where there isn't
a mock turtle or pipe smoking caterpillar in sight.
Here time doesn't stand still for a second,
which is irksome for someone from where
it is permanently tea-time, 6pm to be precise.
While my attire, particularly my top hat, still a snip
at 10/6, makes these odd fish gawp and snigger.
When I tell whoever will listen, that the heartless Queen
will have my head for desertion and Alice will wonder
what's become of me, they pinch themselves
to check they're still awake.

                Caught,
I'm in a courtroom,
                with the Vice Chancellor chanting
and dealing corruption from a snapping pack,
                until I turn turtle.
                                Upside down,
                I am my own inversion,
a version of a tale
                cut from a blind mouse
                                in a doll's house left in the rain.

There's a lesson to be learned
                about love and loss, and
                                I may never find myself again.

LIZ KENDALL

Song of the Slithy Tove

Oh the life of a tove is the life you will see
When you enter the wabe and identify me
For a tove is the creature I am; I am he
I am she I am tove, that is all I shall be.

It's badgering over and lizarding under:
For cheeses I seek, like a corkscrew I plunder
With rummaging, slithering, turning and slinking;
Until I find milk mould I'll search all unblinking.

Rain pools in the sun-dial's face, flat and lipped-shallow;
It's fresher than porter or eau de marshmallow,
So after my cheese I sip water and harken
To 'venturous sounds as the forest leaves darken.

We toves do not add to the mome raths' outgribing,
Our movements are subtle; no slurps on imbibing
Or ear-itching sounds of uncouth mastication
Will toves let fall; silence is our fascination.

So toves gyring and gimbling in silence you'll see
When you enter the wabe and identify me
For a tove is the creature I am; I am he
I am she I am tove, that is all I shall be.

MANDY WILLIS

Grief Through The Looking Glass.

I often plummet down the rabbit hole of loss.
Leaving my sister above, frozen yet gilded.
While falling, I pick out random memories,
mapped out in pictures and empty jars.

It forces surreal encounters, disjointed parts of myself.
At times it's the sweet taste of bitterness,
giant and engulfing.
At others a tiny husk,
reaching for the golden key of happiness, while drowning in tears.

My rictus grin is layered on.
Fading, ethereal, flickering.
Cat-like in its inconsistency.
I create scenarios we never shared.
Us sat together again and again, but with no sustenance.
The cups are empty and the sand refuses to shift the hourglass.

I move on alone.

Bargain with fate.
Negotiate how to redeal the cards.
Change the rules to the game.
Restore my heart.

I rage, view others calmly progressing.
No anxiety for them about it being too late.
I rush into activities chasing time.
Darting manically forwards.
The door through which you passed may open expeditiously via my mad
decisions.

I'm enticed to stay, buffeted by this new reality.
I'm yearning, fighting stubbornly, renouncing the dream.
Dysmorphic in the present.
Observing their sisters.
Screaming internally "Off with their Heads".

CHRISTINE TOKUNAGA

I'm Antarctica Alice, here to welcome you!

Wind, snow and ice
leave patterns on
your windows.
With our fingers,
breath so warm,
we can trace for you
memories of this
cold, cold night!

You're not the only one, Alice, who is here.
I'm Princess Snowdrift from Lapland.
I have a Castle of ice and snow.
I belong here as well as you.
I'm the most beautiful icicle, no one ever leaves me.
Not even you, Alice. From a broken mirror,
I'll place a shard of glass in your eye.

We Penguins live together.
Antarctic Fantastic. Fantastic Antarctica.
We'll tell you facts about Penguins.
Facts you oughta know. Facts you gotta know.
Penguins are birds! Penguins are birds who don't fly.
Emperor Penguins live in Antarctica.
Emperor Penguins walk 70 miles
to find a place to mate and hatch their eggs.
Emperor Penguins go without food
on their long journey.

Excuse me, Sir Penguin, Sir.
I have a small question.
Where did you get your name?
No idea of that. What we want to know,
Alice, is how did you get here?

Floating, floating.
I came here with Mother Hubbard
in her Floating Cupboard!

We're Penguins looking for Oysters and
Sea Snails. Not to eat,
but just to greet!

Where am I from, did you ask?
I've been through the Looking
Glass, so I know all about Mirrors,
broken ones especially.
I can't go home until the slivers of glass in my eye,
disappear from view.
When will that happen?

When I play cards with Sir Humpty Dumpty.
I'll be the Princess of Diamonds, not the Lady of Shards.
Is Sir Humpty here as well, Alice?
Well Penguins, he might be. Such splendid things
happen here in Antarctica.

You said you're Alice. Do you mean Wonderland Alice?
Yes, but Antarctica is the new Wonderland!
So that's why I'm here.

Are you alone?
Oh no, friends from home are here.
Walrus and his Oysters bowing.
The Red Queen, of course.

I'm the Red Queen and you are all my pawns!
I'll help you Alice and you Penguins
when you're out walking.
I'm a Beacon and a Signpost.
Penguins! This way to the Breeding Grounds.
Not too cold. Not too windy.
You and your eggs will be safe if you walk
in that direction (pointing in the opposite direction).

We're ready to start our March. There's just one problem.
We can't agree on our Marching March.

Do you need music?
Yes Alice, we certainly do. It helps us walk so far away.
Music is important. It keeps us warm.
We won't eat for 4 months, you know.
We like our old music.

What's the old music?
The March of the Penguins. We ask you to join us, Alice.
Wait, that's from the Nutcracker, March of the Toy Soldiers.
Not in Antarctica it isn't. Here, it's the Penguins March.
Okay, everyone ready? Let's get marching.

Stop all Penguins!
Yes, Red Queen.
You're off in the wrong direction
and I don't like your Marching Music.
It's for toy soldiers, not Penguins.
You should have a March
from the Southern Hemisphere
where you Penguins live.
Alice, you lead us then.

My feet are so cold! I need feathers too.
Why Alice, haven't you got any?
No, only this thin dress.

Here Alice, we have an extra feather jacket.
Just the thing if you've come from Wonderland.
We're Scientists from the South Pole Research Station.
We're studying Penguins. They don't fly, of course.

Document, document. How many Penguins will survive
blizzards and 4 months without food?
We count all Penguin mothers
returning with fish from the sea.
I'm counting just now.

Wait, don't count us. We're Oysters!
Don't count us either, we're Oyster-Photographers.
We take pictures through holes in our shells.
We Oyster-Photographers document as well,
the Penguins Long March. We'll get perfect shots.
Red Queen, can we take pictures of you?

No time, no time. I'm so busy! Leave me be!
Quiet! I must do my job.

We Oysters have our jobs too. Let us get on with our work.
Working, working through ice and snow.
Walk this way. That way. No, this way is best.

 I believe I should lead. I'm the only Alice here.

Oh no, a BLIZZARD. A BE LIZARD!
What's that? We chick parents see a hole.
Is our chick alive?

Not a hole! Only a cracked egg.
I'm an egg expert. I'm Humpty Dumpty. I know all about eggs,
being one myself of course.

Hey, aren't you the Humpty Dumpty that fell off the wall,
all the King's horses and all the King's men
couldn't put you together again?

What King is that? I'm King here. Do I look like I've fallen off a wall?
Ask these Penguins. I'm King here.
(Penguins nodding) Yes, it's true. He's the King.

Well then. My title, please.
Penguins, shout out!
KING HUMPTY, KING HUMPTY!

Speaking now! This egg has had a bad roll
but it's not frozen yet.
Get it back under your feathers and keep it warm.
Right now!

Are you a Seal?
Me, no! I'm a Walrus.
I'm taking a stroll with these two Oyster friends.
"The time has come...."

Excuse us, dear Walrus.
We Oysters don't want to hear that.
What we want is certainty. Are you going to eat us?
Never! Relax boys. You Oysters are safe with me.

Baby chicks are hatching, hatch, hatched.
Penguin moms have to fish about,
while Penguin dads call out Seal Warnings,
not too late for their mates.

Photographers depart with Princess Snowdrift
to take pictures of her Castle.
Time for King Humpty and Alice to play cards.

Frozen cards? Let's make snow cards and throw them.
I have thrown further than you, King Humpty. I've won!
Now my eye is better, the glass quite gone.

I'm staying here Alice. I fancy being the Exalted Lord of Ice and Snow,
King Humpty of Blizzard and Loss!

Mother Hubbard who lost her Cupboard, and I
Alice, are returning to Wonderland
on an Ice Floe.
Red Queen, how about you?
I'll join you both. I will be missed and needed
beyond all measure.
Of course you will, Red Queen!

So we leave Princess Snowdrift, King Humpty,
Oysters, Penguins, and Photographers,
Scientists, a Walrus and a few references to Seals;
all our new friends, in fact.

Please remember Alice,
shake your tail feathers
and all will be well!